LOVE, IT'S BEATITUDE AND COMPLEXITIES

By

Anthony .UC

INTRODUCTION

This collection is inspired by my desire to share both my happiest and saddest moments in love. To reach out to everyone who may have given up on love after being hurt, to give another shot at it, because love is the most amazing and strongest force on the planet.
It is my hope that you connect with the words and with an open mind let love and happiness into your lives again.

"Behold, thou art fair, my love; behold, thou art fair; thou hast doves' eyes within a thy locks: thy hair is as a flock of goats, that appear b from mount Gilead. [2] Thy teeth are like a flock of sheep that are even shorn, which came up from the washing; whereof every one bear twins, and none is barren among them. [3] Thy lips are like a thread of scarlet, and thy speech is comely: thy temples are like a piece of a pomegranate within thy locks. [4]"

Table of contents

What is love

Love
Is a ripe plum
Growing on a purple tree.
Taste it once
And the spell of its enchantment
Will never let you be.

Love
Is a bright star
Glowing in far Southern skies.
Look too hard
And it's burning flame
Will always hurt your eyes.

Love
Is a high mountain

Stark in a windy sky.
If you
Would never lose your breath
Do not climb too high.

<u>What is love? II</u>

Love is you embodying all five
Youmetaphors and so are my
experiences loving you.

A Flower

A satisfied flower is one whose
petals are about to fall
The most beautiful rose is one
hardly more than
A bud wherein the pangs and
ecstasies of desire are working for
a larger and finer growth

A smile

A smile is such a lovely thing
especially upon your face
Hiding all the sorrows or simply
taking their place.

A word

A kindly spoken word means so
much when from you, it comforts
my weary heart or when I'm
feeling blue.
Put your hand in mine alone, and
peace will fill my mind.

A song

A beautiful song can make our
hearts dance

In pretty fast-paced clips when we
hear

The melody of our lives'
unconquerable grips
Words could lift my spirits and
sweet compassion find

A look

The solemn look in your eyes
Tells so much unsaid words,

Many words that says how you'd
love
and nurture me to the heavens
of bliss and peace

A flower,a smile, a word, a song, a
look –
Seem small little things
But when it's all coming from you
What blessings they bring me.

Not always shall you be what you
are now
You are going forward toward
something great
I am on the way with you.

Now and always

With you, now and always
I am

Bonded to you in emotional bliss,
united in physical rapture,
I realize my dreams and fantasies.

Engulfed in contentment
and satisfaction,
I know heaven in your arms.

My intense hunger nourished,
deep yearnings fulfilled,
I am open to you in total trust.

I love you for what you are, but I love you yet more for what you are going to be.

I love you not so much for your realities as for your ideals.

 I pray for your desires that they may be great, rather than for your satisfactions, which may be so hazardously little.

How we became

Starting off on the wrong foot,
One would never know we'll get
here,
How do some people become so
special?
That you don't see them leaving
you
No matter what

Being so committed to the core,
Deep desire for your growth and
more,
Like one who is wired with love,
All they do is give love,
One with a pure heart and soul,

This is one I know

You're a fine art,
A collection of uniqueness
unparalleled,
A soul so so radiant,
Like the dazzling sun,
You give warmth and light.

At some point this person
Whose core tenets
Molded it's roots
From intelligence.

Whose presence evokes
A vast atmosphere of sage,
Spitting words that nurture dreams
Like a seedling on a nursery bed,
Awakening both gusto and
passion,
Expelling forlorn self doubt

For he is blessed with
Strength that inspires,
Perseverance that infuses
Potency to aspiration.
Yes, a peculiarity of existence.

In my head (Peace)

I think of you in the morning
before the sun rises,
when in the still of the darkness
my heart feels your presence.
Your love, your tenderness,
your slow rhythmic breathing as
you sleep,
and I am at peace.

I think of you when the first rays
of sunlight
spill like a waterfall between the
blinds

and settle in my eyes.
I reach my hand, my foot, any
body part will do,to touch you and
breathe you in.
It feeds my heart, my soul, my
spirit, and I am at peace.

I think of you at noon when the
sun is at its highest,
when the heat warms my skin
and causes my eyes to close with
sheer pleasure.
Thoughts of you surround me,
envelop me, overpower me.
Images of you swirl around like a
funnel cloud,
sucking into its grasp all that it
touches,

and I am at peace.

I think of you when the sun is
setting
and its final rays of light begin to
fade.
I can hear your voice, deep, soft,
and slow in my head--
words of beauty, joy, friendship,
and everlasting love.
My heart begins to sing a love
song so sweet and so gentle.
I cannot wait to share my day with
you and yours with me.
And I am at peace.

I think of you when the sun has set
and the stillness of the moon
is displaying one of its many
wondrous phases.
Thoughts of your smile, your
laugh, and your eyes
create a feeling that is impossible
to express with just words.
The need to touch you, to feel you,
to drink you in
is almost too much to hold inside.
Anticipation of you is the greatest
gift.
I am at peace.

*It all went wrong somewhere
in line
I think we just lost the plot
You never really loved me I
know
And that was never your
thought
So I am moving
With a broken heart
Now the ways are different in
life
It's all far and apart.*

And it happened

Ever felt like your heart's been
snatched from your chest?

Yes, that feeling right there of
shrewd hurt,
That runs through your whole
body like being burnt,

You hear the birds mourn singing
dirges,
For the death of your hopes built
up like ridges,

You were attacked by his charm,
his wits,
His smile, oh! that broad curve
that sits,

On his round, full fleshed, smooth
shiny face,
He looks into your eyes "I love
you" he says,

As his soft small lips forms an arc
of reassurance,
There was no one else but you, not
a chance!

Yet he ripped your heart, now
you're filled with hate,
This is the resignation to your fate,

To be the belly - timber of the
ripper,
Who had once been your lover!

<u>Broken</u>

Once upon a time
I trusted and I loved.
To me, happily ever afters
were totally underrated,

Twas something I believed in,
I gave my heart away,
Only to be returned
Broken, cold and dispirited.

Now I sit in silence
Under this starry sky,
Watching you indulge me afresh
With words of affirmation,

Promises upon promises
Tales of Romeo and Juliet.
You tempt me with the glow
In those firm eyes.

But no! I won't fall,
I had felt this way before
I'd rather you let me be,
To wallow and nurse
My broken self…

Reminisce

Me on the left and you on the right
the way we laid our bodies at the
start of the night.

My head on two pillows as yours
lay on one
tired from the day and all we had
done.

One arm under pillow, the other
kept you warm
I'd pull you in close during
thunder and storm.

I still remember the sweet scent of
your hair

As we closed our eyes and held
each other for warmth.

The rise and fall of breath from
your chest
would remind me of that day that
God had blessed.

Your face would go soft and lips
would yawn
You'd fall asleep with so much
comfort like a baby, my baby.

Middle of the night your house
stayed warm
The fan on high was always the
norm.

Sometimes I'd wake while there
you still lay asleep.
I'd creep to your bedside and just
stare at your beauty

I would lean in close as if to steal
a kiss
These moments of affection are
the ones that I miss.

I'd sit and watch while you lay
there and snore
I'd sometimes fall asleep with my
head on the floor.

Your body lay still except for the
rise and fall
Of your beautiful body that lay
there in sprawl.

But the most memorable part of
those sleepless nights
Wasn't the snoring, the prayer or
absence of lights,

It was the way in which your eyes
would flicker
Beneath the lid and lash I would
try not to snicker.

To me it was funny to just watch
them move

As if they were dancers stepping
to the groove.

I could only guess what your mind
would dream
Maybe thoughts of our future and
how it would seem.

Would it be an uphill battle, a test
for all time?,
Or simply steps in a stairwell that
together we'd climb.

Most of the mornings you'd wake
with a smile
And some you slept in for at least
a little while.

But now these memories are just
written in line
And filed in a cabinet in the back
of my mind.

Memory of you sleeping, snoring,
eyes wide shut
Now my heart is beating,
bleeding, crimson and cut.

Your eyelids would flutter as your
eyes would dance
And I'd pray to God to just give
me the chance

To fix what I'd done and to right
the wrong

Of the poor choices that I'd hidden
for oh so long.

These are the thoughts I now
remember the most
the memories in my heart I still
hold so close.

Times I sat by your side as night
was still grey
All through the morning before
dark turned to day.

I'd ask Him to bless this love I'd
forsaken
Taken for granted and stolen for
the taking.

Unfortunately I received a
different kind of answer
but you will always remain mine.

How could I be so stupid
To let you slip away?
I had you in my arms,
But I let you slip away.

I want you back,
But now it's too late.
I've already said goodbye,
And now love has turned to hate.

I want to go back in time
And fix all that was wrong,
Change all of my actions
So we didn't fight as long for
someone else to show up

And they were all my fault.
I was so immature;

I should have acted like an adult.

I broke my own heart
When I walked out on you.
Now it's seemingly too late,
And I can't undo it.

I still love you,

It was a bad decision,
And now I want you here.
Never far away,
Always near.

So please take me back,
And catch me when I fall
'Cause I need you right now
More than anything at all.

<u>Let Me</u>

Let me take care of your broken
heart
and show you how to fly.
Let me hold you gently by the
hand
and kiss your tears goodbye.

Let me lead you to tomorrow's
light
and out of needless rain,
'cause all I want right now
is to see you smile again.

Let me sing you all the songs I
wrote
'til you sleep in my embrace,
and I'll keep you safe and warm
until
the sunlight strokes your face.

Let me bring you up the
mountain's peak,
and I'll let you touch the skies
to remind you of the strength I see
when I look into your eyes.

Let me kiss and show you what is
love
and the happiness it brings.
You'll sail again like a butterfly
endowed with pretty wings.

Let me do all these to let you see
our fates are intertwined.

The earth and sky conspired to
make us meet.
They knew we both belong
to each other like words and
lovely notes
give life to every song.

So fly with me, my beautiful one.
It's time we leave the past.
I'm yours to keep, and you are
mine.
We're finally home at last.

Nostalgia

When you're away from me
I long for you...
in my thoughts,
in the center of my soul.

I yearn to see
the affection in your eyes...
blue depths of love for me.

I crave the safe warmth
of your arms around me...
my cave of comfort, ease and
peace.

My body aches with hunger for
you…
the exquisite torture
of delayed ecstasy,
coming soon, coming soon.

I long for you, I yearn for you,
I ache for you...
Please, bring all that I crave
in your incomparable self.

Come to me, no "come back" to
me.

Forlorn

Is it really true our love is over
now?
Can it be time for us to say
goodbye?

Too soon, it's much too soon, for
me; You smile with ease, but I can
only sigh.

We've shared our lives and given
so much love; I can't believe we're
really going to part.

Is this me ? God or some force?

You're moving toward a new life
without me;
 I'm left with scars upon my
broken heart.

Now that you're gone, I realize
How much you meant to me.
My loss is wide as a starless night
sky and deep as a stormy sea.

I miss the comfort of your sweet
love, Your absolute devotion.
Now I'm a fountain of endless
tears, a pool of sad emotion.

They tell me I should move on
with life,
That time will heal my pain;

I smile and nod and agree with them,
While I slowly go insane.

Song of Solomon 6:3 KJV

"I am my beloved's, and my
beloved is mine: he feedeth b
among the lilies".

The configuration

Memories upon memories
I reminisce those days,
Of laughter and tears
Of bliss and of my fears
Fear of losing us,
Fear of the uncertainty of us,

Nonetheless,
The future beams with jollity
Because of you
Who makes the road straighter
To help me around each turn
You makes every single day
greater
And soothes whatever hurt

You have taught me,
And I have learnt,
You are teaching me,
And I'm learning,
I hope you'll teach me more,

I have learnt to love differently,
To love enviously,
Revering our beatitude,
I hope we help each other suffer
less,
And grow together in happiness.

My dearest,
You are my muse,
My driving force, my propeller.
Let's journey to forever,
I'd walk with you

Through good and bad,
The rough and the tough,
The thick and the thin.

Our love shall flourish
Like a flower in bloom time.
Together, Let's paint a picture
Of the dazzling beauty of our love,

I'll hold your hand
And guide you as you take
Those frail steps towards loving
again.
You may have given up on love,
But I'm never giving up on you
Not on us.

Beatitude

There's a stream that flows

right through my heart.
It's an endless stream of love
 And affection for you my
Soulmate.

The sounds of music and melody
that makes my heart bubble
have been a part of the music
that your love creates,
this is why I have always loved
you since we met.

In the moments when
My thoughts travel
like the birds in the air,
I catch a glimpse
of how high your love is

and I just feel like making a nest
in your heart.

Love is not one of the precious
stones that men seek.
Love is the only stone!
This is why I am unable to
quantify
the value of your love for me
because it is more precious than
jewelry.

We are lovers created by fate and
destiny
but even more powerful than
predestination

Is the intention you put into
scribbling your name on my heart.
There's nothing that would stop
this flood of emotions from
breaking their banks whenever I
set my eyes on you, so, come
along with a boat!

You are the first thought I
embrace every morning
because out here, the world is cold
but your love feels like the warmth
of a winter blanket.
My heart is made of glass,
so delicate and fragile.
Yet when I see the way you
handle it with your delicate touch,

I am assured that this wine of love
will not be wasted on the cold
floor.
I'd love to show you
how much you mean to me,
but you are everything

so, I'd rather just be the reason
you smile every day.

Song of Solomon 8:6 KJV

Set me as a seal upon thine
heart, as a seal upon thine arm:
for love is strong as death;
jealousy is cruel d as the grave:
the coals e thereof are coals of
fire, which hath a most
vehement flame.